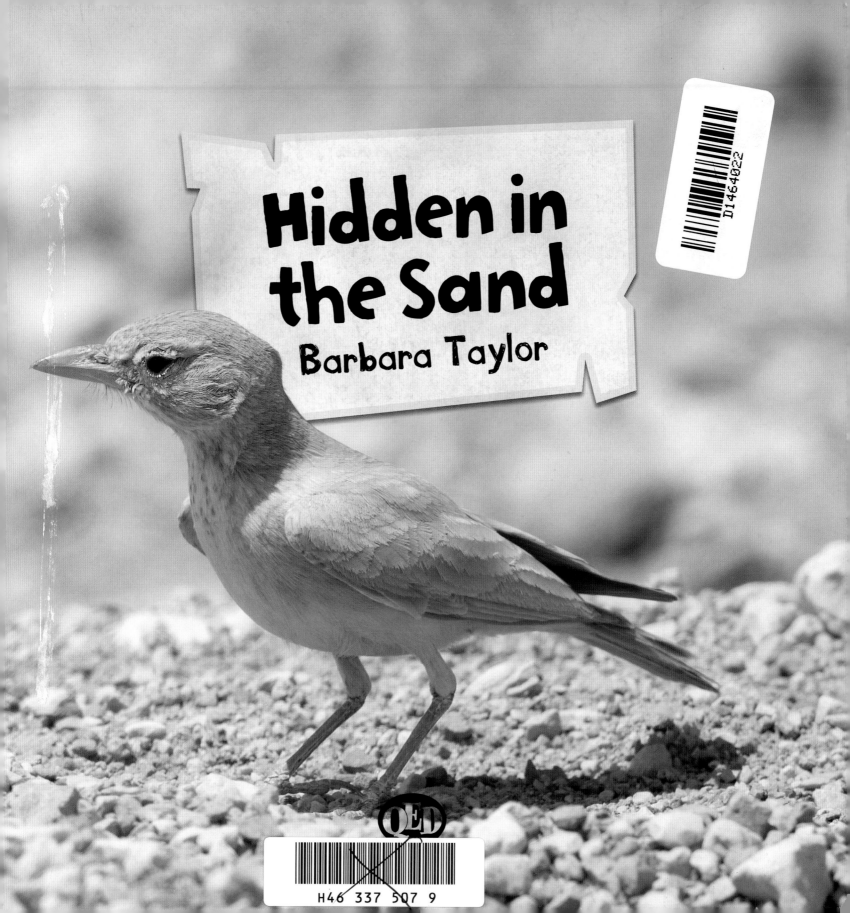

Hidden in the Sand

Barbara Taylor

Project Editor: Angela Royston
Designer: Matthew Kelly
Picture Researcher: Maria Joannou

Copyright © QED Publishing 2011

First published in the UK in 2011 by
QED Publishing
A Quarto Group Company
226 City Road
London EC1V 2TT

www.qed-publishing.co.uk

The words in **bold**
are explained in the
Glossary on page 22.

Front cover: A fennec fox is the
same colour as the sand in the
Sahara Desert, where it lives.

A catalogue record for this book is available from the British Library.

ISBN 978 1 84835 607 8

Printed in China

Picture credits
(t=top, b=bottom, l=left, r=right, c=centre, fc=front cover, bc=back cover)
Corbis Michael & Patricia Fogden 17b, Martin Harvey 20b; **FLPA** Michael & Patricia
Fogden/Minden Pictures 5t, Vincent Grafhorst/Minden Pictures 7bl, Chris Mattison 11,
Sebastian Kennerknecht/Minden Pictures 13t, Scott Linstead/Minden Pictures 13b, Otto
Plantema/Minden Pictures 17t, Piotr Naskrecki/Minden Pictures 20t, Michael & Patricia
Fogden/Minden Pictures 21b; **Nature Picture Library** Simon King 7t, David Tipling 8,
Dr. Gertrud Neumann-Denzau 9b, Michael D. Kern 10–11, Steven David Miller 21t;
Photolibrary MVaresvuo Mvaresvuo 1, 12, Alain Dragesco-Joffé 4, Ingo Schulz 5b, Michel
Gunther 6, Alain Dragesco-Joffé 9t, John Cancalosi 14–15, Superstock/James Urbach
16, Peter Arnold Images/John Cancalosi 19; **Science Photo Library** Gerald C. Kelley 15,
Anthony Mercieca 18; **Shutterstock** Jeffrey M. Frank 2–3, 22–23, 24

Contents

Hiding in the sand

fur the same colour as sand

long legs to run away from hunters

Animals that live in hot, sandy **deserts** are good at hide and seek. The animals hide by blending in with the background. This is called **camouflage.**

Some animals have pale sandy colours, which match the sandy ground. This makes them hard to see. The sandy colour of dorcas gazelles hides them from hunters, such as cats and hyenas.

▲ Dorcas gazelles live in deserts in the mountains of Africa and Arabia.

Spots and blotches

Other animals have patterns, such as spots, streaks or blotches. They are well camouflaged in stony deserts.

Some animals, such as stone grasshoppers, look like stones! A stone grasshopper disappears on the stony ground of its African desert home.

HIDE AND SEEK

A stone grasshopper is hard to see among the stones. Can you spot this one?

eyelids for keeping sand out of the eyes

spotted skin ......>

▲ The spots on the skin of a leopard gecko are just like those on a real leopard's fur.

Sandy animals

Deserts are so dry that few plants can grow there. In sandy deserts, the wind blows the sand into hills called sand dunes. There are not many places to hide!

Many desert animals are pale brown, yellow or silver to give them camouflage. Jerboas usually come out at night. They have a light-brown back to camouflage them during the day.

▶ The jerboa's back camouflages it from hunters. Its white belly reflects, or sends back, the heat of the sand and keeps the jerboa cool.

long tail for balance

long legs to leap away from danger

hairy toes do not sink into the sand

Meerkats

A meerkat's fur is silver, orange or golden brown to match the sand of its desert home. Meerkats hunt for **insects**, spiders and **scorpions** during the day.

Meerkats live together in groups. Some meerkats watch out for animals that hunt them, such as eagles, while the rest of the meerkats play or search for food.

ANIMAL TALK

- Meerkats can see a **bird of prey** even if they are looking into the sun.

- Adult meerkats will sometimes work together to kill a snake.

very good eyesight

▶ Meerkats stand up tall on their back legs to watch out for danger.

strong claws to dig for bugs underground

▼ When danger comes, all the meerkats hide below ground until it is safe to come out again.

Hunting in the sand

Only a few animals can survive in the hot, dry desert. Animals that hunt other animals for food are called **predators**. The animals they hunt are called **prey**.

A roadrunner hunts during the day. Its streaked feathers camouflage it as it hides and waits. When a snake or other prey comes by, the roadrunner leaps out and grabs it.

long tail helps the bird to steer

long legs for running fast

◄ This roadrunner has just caught a snake to eat for dinner!

Hunting at night

Many desert animals hunt at night, when it is cooler. As it gets dark, sand cats come out to hunt for mice, lizards and birds.

During the day, sand cats shelter among the rocks and stones. They crouch low to the ground with their ears flat. Predators such as wolves, snakes and birds cannot see them.

◄ As the sun sets, a sand cat sets off to hunt.

big ears to hear mice moving under the ground

▲ A sand cat has thick fur under its paws to protect them from the burning hot sand.

Snake disguises

▼ A snake's skin is covered with tough, overlapping scales.

Desert snakes wait patiently for a meal to pass by. Their colours and patterns match the sand and rocks. Some desert snakes cover their bodies with sand.

A desert horned viper wriggles its body and sinks under the sand in just a few minutes. Only its head and horns show above the surface.

long poisonous fangs for killing prey

heat pit

Hunting at night

Many desert snakes hunt at night, because it is too hot during the day. Rattlesnakes can find their prey in total darkness. They have two special openings, called pits, below their **nostrils**. These pits pick up the heat of nearby animals.

rattle made of loose scales in tail

SNAKE FACTS

- A rattlesnake makes a buzzing sound when it shakes its tail. This warns predators to keep away.

- Horned vipers make their warning sound by scraping their **scales** together.

▼ A horned viper disappears into the sand. Its scaly horns shade its eyes from the sun.

horn

Hiding from hunters

Prey animals are less likely to be caught if they are hard to find. If they keep still, their camouflage hides them. It gives them a good chance of staying alive.

Desert larks match the sandy colour of desert soil. These tiny birds are hard to see, especially when they sit still on their nest on the ground.

▶ Desert larks that live on lighter coloured sands are paler than those that live on dark sands.

Running away from danger

Jackrabbits and their relatives, desert cottontail rabbits, run fast in a zig-zag pattern to escape from predators. The cottontail's white tail is like a warning flag. It tells other cottontails to run away, too.

A jackrabbit is a type of hare. Its fur is made up of brown hairs with black tips, which help it to hide among thin desert bushes.

▼A jackrabbit's long ears lose heat quickly and so help it to cool down.

ANIMAL TALK

- A jackrabbit can run faster than a racehorse!
- A jackrabbit has eyes on the sides of its head, so it can spot danger from all directions.

long ears to listen for danger

◄ A cottontail rabbit uses its long back legs to run away from danger.

13

Disappearing lizards

Horned lizards search for ants to eat during the day. These tiny lizards are in danger from predators, such as hawks and snakes.

Horned lizards have spiny skin. The colours and patterns on their skin match the sandy background. Horned lizards can also change colour over time to blend in better with their surroundings.

wide, flat body

fringe of scales breaks up outline of body

Vanishing trick

A horned lizard moves slowly. If it has to move, it runs a little way and then stops suddenly. When this lizard flattens its wide, flat body against the ground, it makes no shadow. It just melts into the ground and vanishes.

LIZARD FACTS

- A horned lizard eats several hundred ants every day.

- The lizard's tough skin protects it from the ants' stings.

- Some horned lizards are only 7.5 centimetres long! That's as long as a playing card!

▼ A horned lizard can puff up its body to twice its normal size. This makes it too big for predators to swallow.

Eggs, chicks and babies

▼ A baby gazelle's dull-coloured fur blends in with the grass that grows after it has rained.

Many desert birds lay their eggs on the ground, because there are no trees for their nests. Gazelles and other large animals also have to hide their babies on the ground.

Baby gazelles and antelopes are often a dull brown colour. When they crouch down low and keep still, they look like brown rocks or bumps.

Caring dad

A female sandgrouse lays three spotted eggs on the ground. She keeps the eggs warm during the day and the male takes over at night.

When the eggs hatch, the sandgrouse chicks are well camouflaged. The parent birds often have to fly a long way to find water. The male bird then wets his tummy feathers and carries the water back to the chicks.

▲ A female sandgrouse is well camouflaged against the ground.

▼ Two sandgrouse chicks wait for their parents to bring them water.

Spot the difference

Fennec foxes live in Africa. Kit foxes live in North America. Even though these foxes live in very different parts of the world, it is hard to tell them apart.

A fennec fox and a kit fox look the same because they both live in deserts and use the same skills to survive. The fennec fox has a fluffy, cream-coloured coat, which blends in with its sandy home.

◄ It gets very cold in the desert at night. Then the fennec fox's thick fur keeps it warm.

18

All year round

A kit fox has a thick, furry coat, which is brown or grey in summer. Its fur changes to silvery grey in winter, when there may be snow in the desert.

Kit foxes come out at night to hunt for prey such as kangaroo rats, snakes and jackrabbits.

huge ears for hearing prey

ANIMAL TALK

- A fennec fox digs a **den** below ground. The den can have up to 24 entrances.

- A kit fox is about the same size as a cat.

▼ A young kit fox first leaves the den when it is about four weeks old.

strong legs for leaping up high

Changing colour

Some desert lizards are very good at changing colour to match their background. Patches of colour in their skin move, or become bigger or smaller, to change how the lizard looks.

Desert lizards change colour for many different reasons. A desert chameleon changes colour for camouflage and when it is fighting or frightened. It also changes colour as the day gets hotter or cooler.

▲ A desert chameleon turns green when it is on a green plant...

▶ ...and brown when it is on sand.

Two heads

A thorny devil changes colour from reddish brown to black to match its background. It has a false head behind its real one. If a thorny devil tucks its real head between its legs, a predator will attack the false bump, so the real head is not hurt!

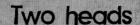

HIDE AND SEEK

Can you see the false head of this thorny devil?

false head

spikes to guard against predators

sticky tongue for catching insects

▲ A thorny devil moves in jerky strides. so that it looks like a leaf blowing in the wind.

Glossary

bird of prey A bird that kills its prey with curved claws, called talons. Birds of prey also eat dead animals.

camouflage Colours, patterns or markings that help an animal to hide by matching the background.

den The home of a wild animal.

desert A large, dry sandy or stony place.

insect A small animal with six legs and three parts to its body.

lizard A small reptile with four legs and a long tail. Chameleons and geckos are different kinds of lizard.

nostril An opening in the nose, through which air can enter the body.

predator An animal that hunts and kills other animals to get food to eat.

prey An animal that is hunted and killed by a predator.

scales Small, thin, dry pieces of skin that overlap.

scorpion A small animal related to spiders. It has nipping claws and a poisonous sting in its tail.

Did you spot them?
On page 5, the stone grasshopper is just below and to the left of the centre of the picture. On page 21, look at the other photo to help you spot the thorny devil's false head.

Index

Notes for parents and teachers

As you share this book with children, ask questions to encourage them to look closely at the photographs and talk about how each animal adapts to its surroundings.

What is sand?
- Sand is mostly made up of tiny pieces of rocks. When sand gets wet it becomes sticky and can be made into shapes such as sandcastles. Encourage children to discover how sand can camouflage objects and animals. Ask the children to lay stones and seashells on the sand, and then see if they can spot them from a distance.

As dry as a desert
- Animals that live in the desert can survive with very little water and get most of their liquid from their food. Remind children that they, however, need to drink lots of water!

Keeping cool
- Deserts can be burning hot by day, but freezing cold at night. Animals often hide underground, or inside cacti, to avoid the heat of the day. They come out at night, when it is cooler and damper.

- Large, thin ears give off heat, and mammals and birds also sweat or pant to keep cool. Ask the children how they cool off when they are too warm.

Moving around
- Camouflage works best when animals keep still, but the hot, shifting sands of a desert make this difficult!
- Ask the children to play camouflage hide and seek! Each child can pick a surface or area they want to blend into and then dress up to match it; for example a white bed sheet in front of a white wall, or brown clothes to match a brown sofa. After the game is finished, the children can vote for their favourite costume and discuss who was the best camouflaged.

Hunters and hunted
- Look through the book and ask the children to find the predators (hunters) and prey (hunted animals). This can be different from one page to the next, as many predators are prey for larger animals! Make a collage to show a food chain. For example, a sand cat hunts lizards, and a lizard hunts for insects.